TEAM SPORTS

The Diagram Group

FRANKLIN WATTS
London ■ New York ■ Sydney ■ Toronto

© Diagram Visual Information 1992

Franklin Watts
96 Leonard Street
London EC2A 4RH

Franklin Watts Australia
14 Mars Road
Lane Cove
NSW 2066

UK ISBN: 0–7496–0882–X

ART DIRECTOR
Darren Bennett

AUTHOR
David Lambert

TYPOGRAPHER
Tim Scrivens

EDITOR
Louise Clairmonte

ARTISTS
James Dallas, Brian Hewson, Lee Lawrence, Ali Marshall, Lee Papworth,
Graham Rosewarne

A CIP catalogue record for this book is available from the British Library

Printed and bound by Toppan Printing, Singapore

CONTENTS

BALL SPORTS
POPULAR BALL SPORTS

Number of Players

1 American Football
This has 11 players a side. One side at a time runs with, passes or kicks an oval ball in short 'plays'. The aim is to win points by touchdowns behind the defence's goal line or by kicking the ball over the goal crossbar. Defenders can tackle the ball carrier. Playing time is 60 minutes with one long interval and two brief ones.

2 Australian Rules Football
Two teams of 18 play on an oval field with four goalposts at each end. Kicking the oval ball between the inner posts scores a goal, between the outer posts, a 'behind'. Besides kicking, players may run with the ball, bouncing it as they go, and make punched hand-passes. Playing time is 100 minutes with three intervals.

3 Gaelic Football
This Irish game has 15 players a side. At each end of the pitch is a goal with a net below the crossbar. Players kick, catch, punch and bounce a round ball. Kicking it under the crossbar scores a goal (3 points). Kicking it over the crossbar scores 1 point. Playing time is 80 minutes, with three intervals.

4 Soccer (Association Football)
Soccer involves two teams of 11 players. Each team tries to kick or head a round ball into the other team's goal. Only the goalkeeper is allowed to handle the ball, although other players may use the chest or thighs. The team that scores the highest number of goals wins. Playing time is 90 minutes, with one interval at half time.

5 Rugby Union
Rugby union is an amateur game for two teams of 15 players who kick, carry and throw an oval ball. Each team tries to score points by placing the ball on or over the other team's goal line (a try) or by kicking over the goal crossbar (a goal). Defenders can tackle the ball carrier. Playing time is 80 minutes, with one interval.

6 Netball

This is for two teams of 7 players. Each team tries to score goals by throwing a round ball into a net above the opposing team's end of the court. Players must stay in fixed areas. They pass by throwing or bouncing the ball but they may not run with it. Playing time is 60 minutes, with three intervals.

7 Volleyball

Two teams of 6 players are separated by a net strung across a court. A team scores points by sending a ball over the net inside the court boundaries so that the opposing team cannot return it. Players may propel the ball with any part of the body above the waist. An international match is decided by the best of five sets.

8 Basketball

Rather like netball, this is a fast game for two teams of 5 players. Each team tries to score goals by throwing a ball into a basket above the opposing team's end of the court. Players do not stay in fixed areas and they may pass, throw, roll, bat or dribble the ball. Professional playing time is 48 minutes, with three intervals.

9 Canadian Football

Canadian football resembles American football but there are 12 players a side. Also the field is larger, with a 'dead-line' 25 yards behind each goal line, and some of the rules are different. For instance, there is an extra means of scoring 1 point. Playing time is 60 minutes with one long interval and two brief ones.

10 Rugby League

Rugby league developed from rugby union. Each match involves two teams of 13 amateur or professional players. Some rugby league rules differ from rugby union ones but, in both games, play is almost continuous and not broken up into short 'plays' (set manoeuvres) as in American football. Playing time is 80 minutes with one half-time interval.

Number of Players

BALL SPORTS
LESS COMMON BALL SPORTS

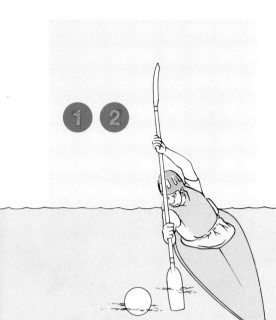

1 Canoe Polo, Open-water
This is a mainly handball sport for two teams of 5 players. Players paddle polo kayaks on a clearly marked-out area of water. They try to score goals by putting the ball through the front of the opponents' goal. Playing time is 60 minutes with one interval.

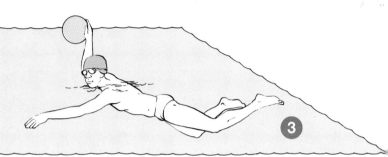

2 Canoe Polo, Indoor
This is similar to open-water canoe polo, but played in swimming pools. It involves a smaller playing area, faster play and more rules against using the paddle. Playing time is also shorter: 20 minutes with one interval.

3 Water Polo
Two teams of up to 13 players take part, but only 7 from each team may be in the water at once. Each team tries to score goals by putting the ball in its opponents' net. The players may propel the ball one-handed but only a goalkeeper is allowed to punch it. Playing time is 28 minutes with three brief intervals.

Number of Players

4 Touchball
Two teams of 9 players try to score touchdowns behind their opponents' goal line. They may catch and carry the oval ball and pass it back, but not kick it. A player must give up the ball if touched on the back by an opponent. Playing times are 60 minutes for men and 40 minutes for women, both with three intervals.

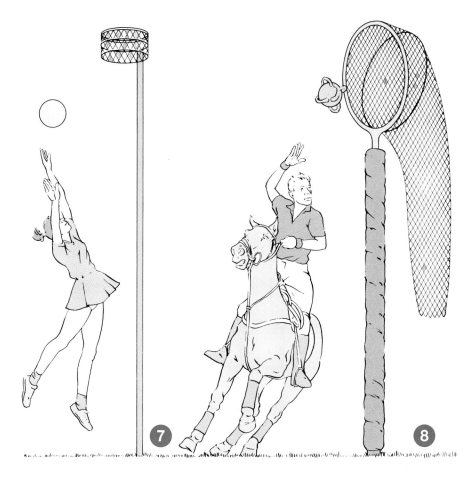

8 Pato

This is a modified version of polo and played mainly by wealthy men. It is an Argentinian net-scoring game and is played on horseback by two teams of 4 riders. They use a round ball with six leather handles, and their goals are windsock-shaped nets fixed high up on posts. Players try to seize the ball and carry it down the field before tossing it into the opposing team's net. The playing time is 48 minutes, with five intervals, each lasting for 4 minutes.

Number of Players

5 Team Handball

This is one of the fastest team games. Two teams of 7 players (and 5 substitutes) try to score goals with a ball like a small soccer ball. Players catch, stop, bounce, throw or strike the ball using hands, fists, arms, head, body, thighs or knees. They may not kick the ball or carry it for more than three steps without bouncing it. When a team gains possession, the other team forms up to defend its goal area. Playing time is 60 minutes with one interval.

6 Speedball

Speedball combines features of such team sports as soccer and basketball. The two teams of 11 men or 11 women may kick, head, throw and catch the ball. How they play it depends on whether the ball is in the air or on the ground. Players may not carry it or charge one another. They score points by making touchdowns behind the opponents' goal line or by kicking the ball over or under the goalposts. Rules of play differ slightly for men and women. Playing time is 40 minutes with one long interval and two brief ones.

7 Korfball

The usual version has 4 men and 4 women in each team and a pitch that is divided into two zones. Half of each team starts in a different zone and players try to score goals by lobbing the ball into a basket fixed high up on a goalpost in their opponents' zone. Players catch and pass the ball with their hands. They may not run with the ball, even when bouncing it, or throw for a goal when blocked by a defender. Playing time is 60 minutes with one interval.

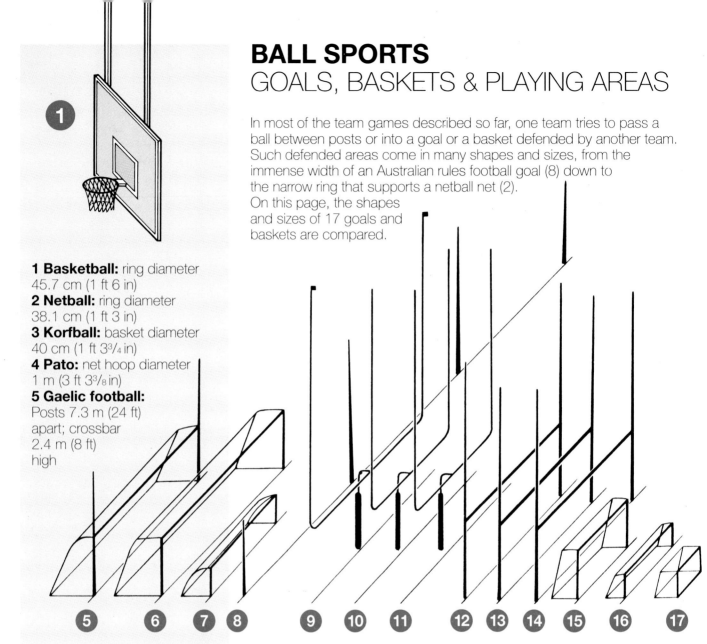

BALL SPORTS
GOALS, BASKETS & PLAYING AREAS

In most of the team games described so far, one team tries to pass a ball between posts or into a goal or a basket defended by another team. Such defended areas come in many shapes and sizes, from the immense width of an Australian rules football goal (8) down to the narrow ring that supports a netball net (2). On this page, the shapes and sizes of 17 goals and baskets are compared.

1 Basketball: ring diameter 45.7 cm (1 ft 6 in)
2 Netball: ring diameter 38.1 cm (1 ft 3 in)
3 Korfball: basket diameter 40 cm (1 ft 3³/₄ in)
4 Pato: net hoop diameter 1 m (3 ft 3³/₈ in)
5 Gaelic football: Posts 7.3 m (24 ft) apart; crossbar 2.4 m (8 ft) high

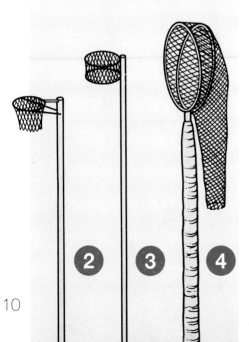

6 Soccer: posts 7.3 m (24 ft) apart; crossbar 2.4 m (8 ft) high
7 Canoe polo (open-water): posts 4 m (13 ft 1 in) apart
8 Australian rules football: outer posts 19.2 m (63 ft) apart; the inner posts are 6.4 m (20 ft 4 in) apart
9 American football (amateur): upper posts 7.1 m (23 ft 4 in) apart and 6.1 m (20 ft) high; crossbar 3 m (10 ft) high
10 American football (professional): upper posts 5.6 m (18 ft 6 in) apart and 9.2 m (30 ft) high; crossbar (see 9)
11 Canadian football: upper posts 5.6 m (18 ft 6 in) apart and 9.2 m (30 ft) high; crossbar (see 9)

12 Rugby union: posts 5.6 m (18 ft 4 in) apart; crossbar 3 m (9 ft 10 in) high
13 Rugby league: posts and crossbar as for rugby union
14 Speedball: posts 5.6 m (18 ft 6 in) apart; crossbar 2.4 m (8 ft) high
15 Team handball: posts 3 m (9 ft 9 in) apart; crossbar 2 m (6 ft 6 in) high
16 Water polo: posts 3 m (9 ft 9 in) apart; crossbar 91.5 cm (3 ft) above water
17 Canoe polo (indoor): a basket 1.5 m (4 ft 11 in) wide and 1 m (3 ft 3 in) high, suspended 2 m (6 ft 6 in) above the water line.

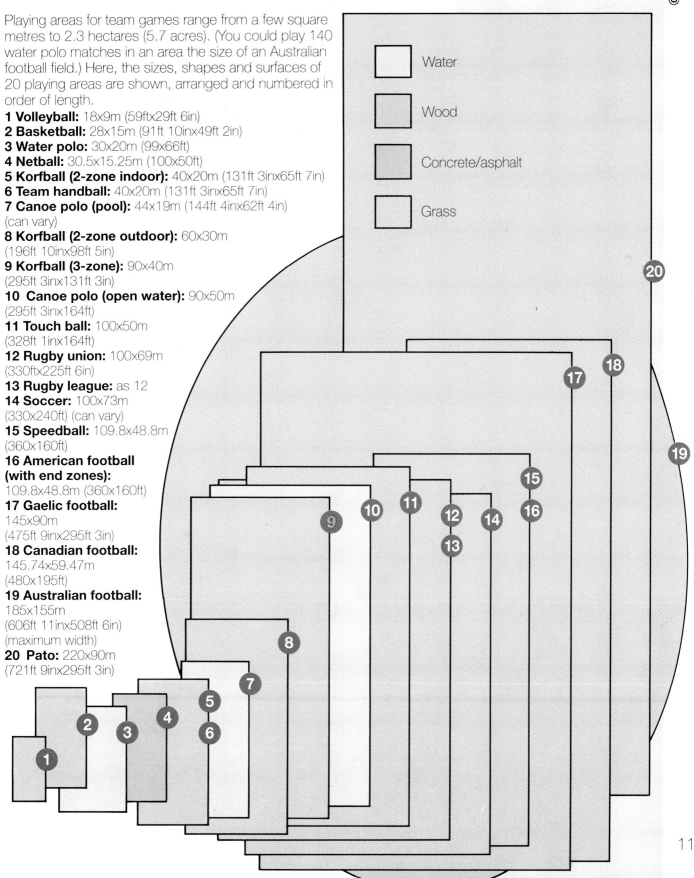

Playing areas for team games range from a few square metres to 2.3 hectares (5.7 acres). (You could play 140 water polo matches in an area the size of an Australian football field.) Here, the sizes, shapes and surfaces of 20 playing areas are shown, arranged and numbered in order of length.

1 Volleyball: 18x9m (59ftx29ft 6in)
2 Basketball: 28x15m (91ft 10inx49ft 2in)
3 Water polo: 30x20m (99x66ft)
4 Netball: 30.5x15.25m (100x50ft)
5 Korfball (2-zone indoor): 40x20m (131ft 3inx65ft 7in)
6 Team handball: 40x20m (131ft 3inx65ft 7in)
7 Canoe polo (pool): 44x19m (144ft 4inx62ft 4in) (can vary)
8 Korfball (2-zone outdoor): 60x30m (196ft 10inx98ft 5in)
9 Korfball (3-zone): 90x40m (295ft 3inx131ft 3in)
10 Canoe polo (open water): 90x50m (295ft 3inx164ft)
11 Touch ball: 100x50m (328ft 1inx164ft)
12 Rugby union: 100x69m (330ftx225ft 6in)
13 Rugby league: as 12
14 Soccer: 100x73m (330x240ft) (can vary)
15 Speedball: 109.8x48.8m (360x160ft)
16 American football (with end zones): 109.8x48.8m (360x160ft)
17 Gaelic football: 145x90m (475ft 9inx295ft 3in)
18 Canadian football: 145.74x59.47m (480x195ft)
19 Australian football: 185x155m (606ft 11inx508ft 6in) (maximum width)
20 Pato: 220x90m (721ft 9inx295ft 3in)

Water
Wood
Concrete/asphalt
Grass

Netball

Players wear shirts or blouses, skirts or shorts, socks and shoes which must not be spiked. They use a size 5 soccer ball made of leather or rubber, and weighing 400–450 g (14–16 oz).

Volleyball

Players wear numbered jerseys and shorts in team colours (outdoors, tracksuits if it is cold), and light heelless shoes. They use a leather or rubber ball of 65–67 cm (25½–26½ in) in circumference.

Basketball

Players wear numbered shirts and shorts, with basketball boots or sneakers. They use a ball with a leather, rubber or synthetic outer casing. It is 75–78 cm (29½–30¾ in) in circumference.

Korfball

Teams wear distinctive uniforms with shoes, but no objects that could injure someone during the game. They use a ball similar to a soccer ball, of 68–71 cm (26⅔–28 in) in circumference.

Pato

Players dress like polo players, in coloured shirts, white breeches and black riding boots. They use a ball the same size as a soccer ball, but which has six leather handles.

BALL SPORTS
DRESS & PLAYING EQUIPMENT

American and Canadian Football

Players wear the following clothing and protective gear.
1 Plastic helmet
2 Plastic face mask with rounded edges or edged with rubber-covered wire

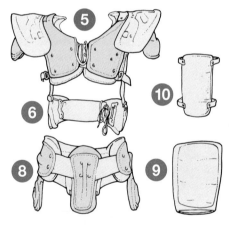

3 Jersey in the team colour which must differ from the ball's colour
4 Numbers on chest and back
5 Chest and shoulder padding
6 Rib and kidney padding
7 Pants
8 Below the belt padding
9 Thigh padding
10 Shin padding
11 Lightweight boots
Players use an oval ball with a leather case, 28–28.6 cm (11–11¼ in) long. The ball weighs 400–425 g (14–15 oz).

Rugby (Union and League)

Players wear jerseys, shorts, socks and boots. League players may wear protective items besides the two kinds shown here.
1 Scrum cap
2 Shin guard
3 Boots with studded soles
Players use an oval ball with a case of leather or other approved material. It is 28 cm (11 in) long and weighs 400–440 g (14–15½ oz).

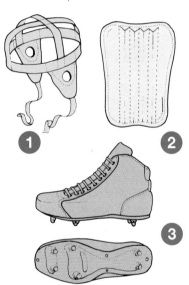

Australian Rules Football

Players wear jumpers, shorts, socks and studded boots. The oval ball has a long circumference of 74 cm (29 in). It weighs 450–475 g (16–17 oz).

Gaelic Football

Players wear shirts, shorts, socks and boots. They use a round leather ball of 69–74 cm (27–29 in) in circumference. It weighs 312–425 g (11–15 oz).

Soccer

See page 16 for dress. A ball of leather or other approved material is used, 69–71 cm (27–28 in) in circumference and weighing 400–450 g (14–16 oz).

Team Handball

Players wear no protective clothing. Goalkeepers must be distinguishable from the other players. All wear shirts with the backs numbered 1–12. Only the goalkeepers use numbers 1 and 12. The ball has a coloured leather casing. Its circumference is 57–60 cm (22²/₃–23¹/₂ in) and weighs 425– 475 g (15–17 oz) for men, and 54–56 cm (21¹/₃–22 in), weighing 325–400 g (11–14 oz), for women.

Canoe Polo

Players are numbered and wear safety helmets and buoyancy aids. Team members have helmets, body covering and kayaks of the same colours.
Kayaks are 2–3 m (6 ft 6 in – 9 ft 10 in) long and up to 50–60 cm (19³/₄–23²/₃ in) wide. They weigh at least 7 kg (15 lb 6 oz). Each player has a double-bladed paddle with no sharp or dangerous features. Open-water canoe polo players use a water-polo ball 69–71 cm (27–28 in) in circumference. Indoor canoe-polo players use a slightly smaller ball.

Water Polo

Players wear bathing costumes and must not oil or grease their skin. One team wears blue caps, the other white. Goalkeepers wear red caps. Caps are tied under the chin and numbered 1–13. Only the goalkeeper bears the number 1. The water-polo ball is 68–71 cm (26⁴/₅–28 in) in circumference and it weighs 400–450 g (14–16 oz). It must be completely waterproof.

Touchball

Players of touchball or 'Finnish rugby' wear shorts and studded boots similar to those used by rugby league or union players. Touchball players also use an oval ball similar to the ball that rugby players use.

Speedball

Speedball players wear uniforms of jerseys and shorts, with football boots. They may not wear equipment likely to cause injury. The ball is an official soccer ball, although a basketball is allowed on a small pitch.

Ball Sizes

1 Basketball
2 Gaelic football
3 Speedball
4 Korfball
5 Soccer
6 Netball
7 Canoe polo (open-water)
8 Water polo
9 Canoe polo (indoor)
10 Volleyball
11 Team handball (men)
12 Rugby union
13 Rugby league
14 Touchball
15 Australian rules football
16 Team handball (women)
17 American football
18 Canadian football

©DIAGRAM

Pato

Six handles made of leather stick out from this unusual ball.

13

BALL SPORTS
SOCCER (ASSOCIATION FOOTBALL)

Soccer is the most popular sport on Earth. More than 140 nations play it and millions of people watch it live or on television.

People have enjoyed football for 2000 years, but early games were more like battles. There were no proper pitches, or rules, until Cambridge University, England, produced a list in 1846. In 1863, the Football Association (FA) was formed. This laid down the rules of association football, or soccer, for teams all over England. In 1871, for the first time, clubs competed for the FA Cup. In 1872, Scotland and England played the first official international match. In 1885, the FA began to allow teams to pay their players. In 1888, English clubs formed the Football League.

By 1900, other countries were playing soccer too. In 1904 in Paris, the Fédération Internationale de Football Association (FIFA) was formed. Soccer appeared in the Olympic Games in 1908, and the great World Cup competition began in 1930.

Dress and Safety

All players wear the items numbered 1–4 and either item 6 or 7. The goalkeeper is the only team member not in team colours.

1 Numbered shirt
2 Shorts
3 Socks
4 Studded or astroturf boots
5 Goalkeeper's gloves
6 Shin pads

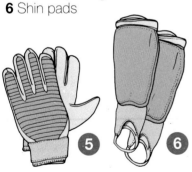

7 Astroturf boots. These are designed for the artificial playing surface, astroturf.

The Pitch

The ends of the pitch are marked by the goal lines. Its sides are marked by the touchlines. Play starts in the centre circle and stops if the ball crosses a touchline or a goal line. Each end has a goal and a goal area with a penalty area outside it. If a defender breaks certain rules here, an attacker may shoot at goal from the penalty spot.

Parts of a pitch

a Touchline
b Goal line
c Goal
d Goal area
e Penalty area
f Penalty spot
g Penalty arc
h Centre circle
i Corner flag

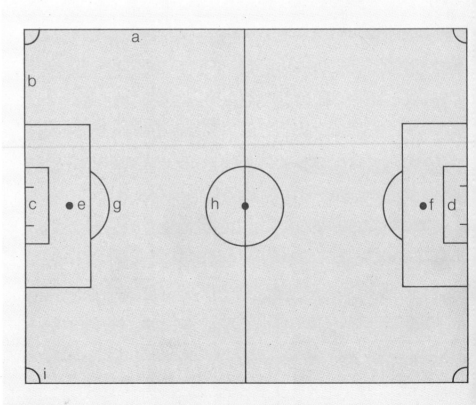

The World Cup

This is the world's greatest soccer championship. It is held every four years and all the nations that belong to FIFA may take part. Two years before the finals, groups of nations from different parts of the world play each other in qualifying rounds. The best go on to take part in the finals. There are usually 16 finalists. They include the country where that year's finals are played, and the cup holders.

The first World Cup trophy was a gold cup called the Jules Rimet trophy. It was named after the president of FIFA who helped to start the World Cup competition. In 1970, Brazil kept this cup for good after winning it three times out of four. West Germany first won the new 'World Cup' in 1974.

World Cup winners
3 Brazil 1958, 1962, 1970
3 West Germany 1954, 1974, 1990
3 Italy 1934, 1938, 1982
2 Argentina 1978, 1986
2 Uruguay 1930, 1950
1 England 1966

Top European Clubs

The top European clubs play one another in knockout competitions organized by the Union of European Football Associations (UEFA). The main contests are
1 European Champion Clubs' Cup
2 European Cup-Winners' Cup
3 UEFA Cup
4 European Super Cup
The map above shows the homes of 15 European clubs.
1 Celtic (Scotland)
2 Rangers (Scotland)
3 Liverpool (England)
4 Manchester United (England)
5 Nottingham Forest (England)
6 Tottenham Hotspur (England)
7 Arsenal (England)
8 Ajax (Netherlands)
9 AC Milan (Italy)
10 Inter-Milan (Italy)
11 Bayern Munich (Germany)
12 Benfica (Portugal)
13 Real Madrid (Spain)
14 Barcelona (Spain)
15 Marseille (France)

Liverpool FC

Liverpool Football Club is one of the most successful clubs in Europe.
By 1991, it boasted these results.
1 Super Cup: 1 win from 3 finals
2 European Cup: 4 wins out of 5 finals
3 UEFA Cup: 2 wins out of 2 finals
4 League Cup: 4 wins out of 6 finals
5 FA Cup: 4 wins out of 9 finals
6 League champions 18 times
7 Second Division champions: four times
8 European Cup-Winners' Cup: reached one final, which they lost
9 Barclays Manager of the Year Award 11 times since 1966: Bob Paisley (6), Bill Shankly (1), Kenny Dalglish (3) and Joe Fagan (1) (Paisley's 9-year reign was the most successful in British soccer history)
10 Many times producer of the player of the year

15

BALL SPORTS
HALL OF FAME

Harlem Globetrotters

This became the world's best-known basketball team, famous for the speed and entertaining antics of its tall players. One of their tricks is spinning the ball on a finger tip. Another is rolling the ball from one hand, up an arm, across the chest and down the other arm to the other hand.

This team gets the first part of its name from an area of New York City. Yet it was started (in 1927) in Chicago. The other name "Globetrotters" is meant to give the idea that the members are world-class players.

At first, the Globetrotters just toured the midwestern states of the United States. In 1940, they won the World Championship for the first time. They made their first European tour in the 1950s. By then they were world famous. One story even tells of how a civil war in Peru was temporarily stopped so that the team could visit in safety.

Michael Jordan

In 1987, this Chicago Bulls player became professional basketball's highest scoring guard, and the world's most highly paid team athlete in 1988.

Walter Payton

Walter 'Sweetness' Payton has been called the greatest-ever American football player. Between 1975 and 1987, he gained more yards both in a game and a career than anyone else and altogether broke 13 National Football League (NFL) records.

Payton claimed his rock-hard hand-off came from boyhood football in the street. There, he had fiercely fended off defenders because he had been scared his mother would be angry if he tore his clothes.

Dickerson and Bennett

In 1984, Eric Dickerson set a new single season rushing record with 2,105 yards. In the late 1980s, Cornelius Bennett became famous for his fast and furious defence.

Elway and Montana

In 1983, quarterback John Elway became the NFL's most highly paid rookie (new recruit). Joe Montana earned his third Super Bowl winner's ring in 1989.

Rob Andrew

All-rounder Rob Andrew captained Cambridge University at cricket and, in 1989, led England's rugby team against Romania. As fly-half, he played more times for England than anyone else before him.

Other Rugby Stars

In 1988, Will Carling became England's youngest captain for 50 years. In 1986, Gavin Hastings set a Scottish first-season record with 14 penalties and 52 points.

Pelé

Many experts think that this Brazilian was the greatest soccer player of all time. Pelé was born in 1940 as Edson Arantes do Nascimento. How he got his nickname is unclear, but there are no doubts about his long and brilliant career.

Pelé became famous for skilful dribbling, superb passing and deadly shooting at goal. While aged only 17, he scored two goals for Brazil in the 1958 World Cup final. Pelé went on to become the only soccer player to perform with three world championship teams and to gain three winner's medals. Altogether, he played in 1,363 professional matches and scored 1,281 goals. Pelé finally retired in 1977, at the age of 37.

Diego Maradona

Brilliant ball control made this short, stocky Argentinian the world's top soccer player of the 1980s. Opponents feared his long, accurate passes, his skill at weaving a ball at high speed between defenders, and his fast accurate shots at goal. In 1986, Maradona led Argentina to World Cup victory in Mexico.

Johan Cruyff

This Dutch player was one of soccer's all-time 'greats'. In the 1960s and 1970s, he baffled opponents with his speed, sharp body swerve and deft footwork.

Other Great Soccer Players

This list includes just 12 of the soccer stars of recent times.
Franz Beckenbauer (West Germany)
Bobby Charlton (England)
Kenny Dalglish (Scotland)
Eusebio (Portugal)
Paul Gascoigne (England)
Ruud Gullit (Holland)
Kevin Keegan (England)
Gary Lineker (England)
Bobby Moore (England)
Michel Platini (France)

Goal Points Averages

Here, the 10 National Basketball Association (NBA) basketball players, with the highest goal points averages up to 1990, are listed. (A goal points average is the number of points scored in a career, divided by the number of games played.)

1 Michael Jordan: 32.8
2 Wilt Chamberlain: 30.1
3 Elgin Baylor: 27.4
4 Jerry West: 27.0
5 Bob Pettit: 26.4
6 Dominique Wilkins: 26.0
7 Oscar Robertson: 25.7
8 George Gervin: 25.1
9 Adrian Dantley: 25.0
10 Larry Bird: 24.9

Soccer World Cup Final Goals

	F	A	W
West Germany	11	13	3
Brazil	13	6	0
Italy	10	8	3
Argentina	8	8	2
Uruguay	6	3	2
Holland	2	5	0
Czechoslovakia	2	5	0
Hungary	4	7	0
England	4	2	1
Sweden	2	5	0

(F = For A = Against W = Wins)

Argentina are the only World Cup finalists to have scored nil in a World Cup Final. They lost 0–1 to West Germany in 1991.

BALL SPORTS
WOULD YOU BELIEVE?

These pages list some outstanding ball sports facts and feats involving teams and individual players. Besides successes, we include one list of resounding defeats and a famous fluke soccer goal scored more than a quarter of a century ago.

Football First

Australian rules football rules are the world's oldest surviving football code, published in 1859. Soccer's rules did not appear until 1863. Rugby and American football rules date from 1871, and Gaelic football rules from 1884.

Michel Platini

This outstanding French soccer player led France to victory in the European Championship in 1984. He was voted European Footballer of the Year three times (1983–85) and became the manager of France in 1988.

Super Bowl Super Losers

In the 1970s, Minnesota Vikings lost four out of the four contests they played in the annual match between the American Football Conference (AFC) and National Football Conference (NFC) champions. Their losing record:
1970 7–23 v. Kansas City Chiefs
1974 7–24 v. Miami Dolphins
1975 6–16 v. Pittsburgh Steelers
1977 14–32 v. Oakland Raiders
By 1990, the Denver Broncos had also lost four out of the four Super Bowls in which they took part (1978, 1987, 1988, 1990).

Super Bowl Super Winners

Pittsburgh Steelers won four out of four Super Bowls by 1980:
1975 16–4 v. Minnesota Vikings
1976 21–17 v. Dallas Cowboys
1979 35–31 v. Dallas Cowboys
1980 31–19 v. Los Angeles Rams
By 1990, San Francisco 49ers had also won four out of the four Super Bowls in which they played (1982, 1985, 1989, 1990).

Franz Beckenbauer

This German sportsman became the only soccer player to win the FIFA World Cup as player/captain and then as manager. In 1974, he led West Germany to victory over Holland, and in 1990 he managed the team that beat Argentina. When he played for Bayern Munich, he was voted European footballer of the year in 1972 and 1976.

Hawthorn 'Hawks'

In Australian rules football, the Hawthorn 'Hawks' became the team to beat in the 1990s. In the 1980s, they had won the Victoria Football League (VFL) four times: in 1983, 1986, 1988 and 1989, and had been runners up in 1984, 1985 and 1987.

World Cup Rugby

New Zealand won the first Rugby Union World Cup in 1987 and produced the highest scoring player of the tournament. New

The Goalie's Goal

One of the most amazing soccer goals ever scored happened in a 1967 Charity Shield match between Manchester United and Tottenham Hotspur. Spurs' goalkeeper, Pat Jennings, cleared the ball from his penalty area with a great kick. The ball soared over the players' heads into Manchester's penalty area. There, it bounced over the Manchester goalie's head straight into Manchester's goal.

Zealand goalkicker Grant Fox scored 126 points in six games: an amazing average of 21 points a game.

Record Soccer Transfer Fees

1 Roberto Baggio: £7.7 million (Fiorentina to Juventus, 1990)
2 Diego Maradona: £6.9 million (Barcelona to Napoli, 1984)
3 Ruud Gullit: £5.5 million (PSV Eindhoven to AC Milan, 1987)
4 Karl-Heinz Riedle: £5.5 million (Werder Bremen to Lazio, 1990)
5 Thomas Hässler: £5.5 million (FC Cologne to Juventus, 1990)
6 Paul Gascoigne: £5.5 million (Tottenham Hotspur to Lazio, 1991–92)
7 David Platt: £5 million (Aston Villa to Bari, 1990)
8 Diego Maradona: £4.8 million (Boca Juniors to Barcelona, 1982)

Grand Slam

Five countries compete in the international Rugby Union championship. England became the first country to win 10 times: 1913, 1914, 1921, 1923, 1924, 1928, 1957, 1980, 1991, 1992.

Champions of Europe

The European Cup is an annual soccer knockout contest between league champions from all the countries belonging to the Union of European Football Associations (UEFA). It began in 1956. Here, all the winning countries and their teams, from 1956 to 1991, are listed.

England 8
Liverpool 4, Manchester Utd. 1
Notts. Forest 2, Aston Villa 1

Italy 7
Juventus 1, AC Milan 4,
Inter-Milan 2

Spain 6
Real Madrid 6

Holland 5
Ajax 3, PSV Eindhoven 1
Feyenoord 1

West Germany 4
Bayern Munich 3,
SV Hamburg 1

Portugal 3
Benfica 2, FC Porto 1

Others
Romania 1 (Steaua Bucharest)
Yugoslavia 1 (Red Star Belgrade)
Scotland 1 (Celtic)

BAT AND BALL SPORTS
POPULAR BAT & BALL SPORTS

1

2

Number of Players

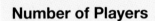

1 Baseball
There are two teams of 9 players. One side bats while the other fields. Each batter tries to strike a ball, pitched to him by a pitcher, and then run between four bases bounding the so-called infield. A batter scores a run by completing one circuit of the bases. Fielders try to put out batters and runners by catching a struck ball or tagging (touching) a runner with the ball outside a base. When the fielding team has put out three of the batting team, the batting side is out and becomes the fielding side. Play lasts for up to nine innings per team. An inning is one side's turn at batting.

2 Ice Hockey
In this sport, both teams are allowed 5 players and a goalkeeper on the ice at any one time. They skate on an ice rink. Players use sticks to try to hit a flat round object called a puck into their opponents' goal. Play starts with a face-off where the referee or linesman drops the puck on the ice between the sticks of two players from opposing sides. Players pass and shoot at goal by sliding the puck along the ice. Goalkeepers try to block shots. Ice hockey is fast, often with many penalties awarded for fouls. Playing time is 60 minutes, with two 20-minute intervals.

3 Softball
Softball began in 1887, in Chicago, as an indoor version of baseball. It is played in a smaller area than baseball and the action is faster. Softball has become a major outdoor team game, played by men and women. There are two types of softball: fast pitch (FP) and soft pitch (SP). Each FP team has 9 players. Each SP team has 10 players. Pitchers and catchers stand in special positions, but the other players may stand anywhere on what is called fair ground. Each game has seven innings per team but all these usually take less than an hour to complete.

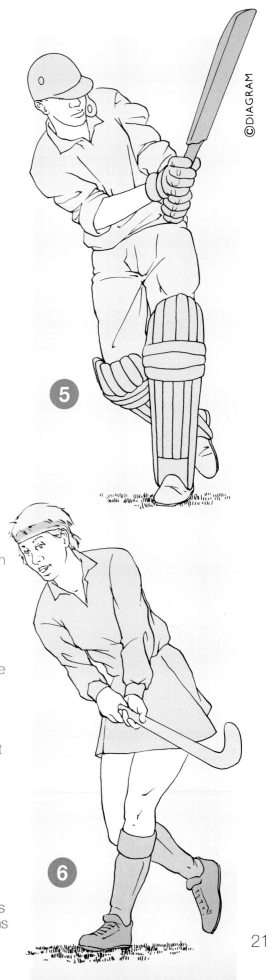

©DIAGRAM

4 Rounders

Rounders is an English game similar to baseball and softball. One team fields while another bats. The batters take it in turns to try to hit a ball and score a rounder. A batter scores by running around four posts without stopping. The batter can stop at any post and be safe. But the batter is out if a fielder catches the struck ball, or touches the batter with the ball while the batter is running, or touches the post that the batter is running toward. The team that scores the most rounders wins. Each team has two innings. An inning ends when a batting team is out.

5 Cricket

Cricket is played mainly in Commonwealth countries. There are two teams of 11 players. One fields while the other bats. Batsmen guard the two wickets, one at each end of a pitch. A bowler at one end of the pitch bowls a small hard ball six times at the far wicket. Then another bowler bowls six balls from the opposite end, and so on. Bowlers try to dismiss batsmen by hitting the wickets or in other ways. Batsmen try to score runs by running between wickets without being bowled or caught out. In a test match, each team has two innings. The team scoring the highest number of runs wins.

6 Field Hockey

Two teams of 11 men or women use sticks with a hooked head to hit a small hard ball along the ground. Each team tries to hit the ball into the other team's goal. Players may control the ball only with the flat side of their own sticks. In the circle around the goal, the goalkeeper may kick the ball or use their pads. If play stops it may be restarted by a 'bully', where the ball is, put on the ground between two players, who tap sticks and then try to hit it. The team scoring the greatest number of goals wins the match. Play lasts 70 minutes with one interval of 5–10 minutes.

BAT AND BALL SPORTS
LESS COMMON BAT & BALL SPORTS

Number of Players

1 Polo
Polo is played by two teams of 4 players on horseback. Each player controls a polo pony with the left hand and uses the right hand to grasp a stick with a mallet head. Players try to score goals by striking a ball between the opposing team's goalposts. Play lasts 56 minutes and is divided into eight 7-minute periods called chukkas.

2 Men's Lacrosse
Lacrosse is a team game where players use a net on a hooked stick to catch, carry and throw a ball. They try to score goals by passing the ball over their opponents' goal line. Men's lacrosse is a 10-a-side game in which players may charge an opponent. A men's lacrosse match lasts 100 minutes, with three intervals.

3 Puck Roller Hockey
This is played by two teams of 5 using sticks and roller skates. The players play with a flat round object called a puck. They score goals by knocking the puck into their opponents' goal net. Play lasts for 40 minutes with one interval. There are no international matches.

4 Ball Roller Hockey
This resembles ice hockey but it is played on roller skates, with a ball. Two teams of 5 players play the ball with their sticks and may stop it with any part of the body. A team scores goals by hitting the ball into the other team's net. Playing time in international matches is 40 minutes with one interval.

5 Cycle Polo
Cycle polo is rather like polo. There are several versions, but instead of riding on ponies, the players ride bicycles. Each team has 5 players using long-handled mallets to hit the ball. They try to score by hitting the ball into the opposing team's goal. A cycle polo match lasts 90 minutes with five intervals.

6 Shinty

Shinty is a Gaelic field game that started in Scotland. There are two teams of 12 men. Players try to score goals by hitting a ball with a club called a caman. They may pass the ball on the ground or through the air, but only a goalkeeper may touch the ball with his hands. Playing time lasts 90 minutes, with one interval.

7 Women's Lacrosse

Women's lacrosse is much like men's lacrosse but with certain differences. The two teams have 12 players each. They play on a larger pitch than the men. Players may not charge one another, and the penalty for all fouls is giving the ball to the fouled player. Playing time lasts 50 minutes, with one interval.

8 Bandy

Bandy is rather like ice hockey. The ice rink is larger. Each team may deploy 11 players at once. Curved sticks are used to hit a ball. There is no play behind goals. If an attacker hits the ball over the opposing team's goal line the goalkeeper may throw the ball back into play. Play lasts 90 minutes with one interval.

9 Hurling

Two teams of 15 players play this Gaelic field game. They hit or carry the ball with curved sticks called hurleys, and kick it or hit it with the hand when it is off the ground. Sending it under the goal crossbar scores 3 points (a goal). Over the bar between posts scores 1 point. Play lasts 70 minutes with one interval.

10 Camogie

This is an Irish field game for women. It is rather like hurling but not so rough as there is less body contact. There are two teams of 12 players. Each team tries to score by sending the ball over or under the crossbar of the other team's goal. The team with the highest score wins. Play lasts 50 minutes with one interval.

Number of Players

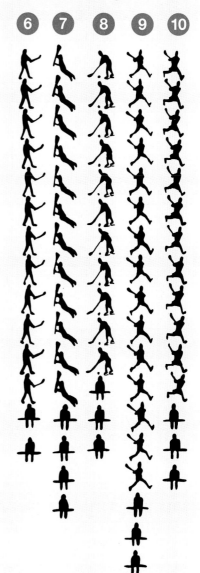

©DIAGRAM

23

BAT AND BALL SPORTS
GOALS, BATTING & PLAYING AREAS

This page shows the goals, bases and wickets used in the 16 bat and ball sports described in the previous four pages. In most of the games, scoring involves hitting a ball into a goal. In run-scoring games, members of the batting team start at one base or wicket and score by running to other bases or another wicket.

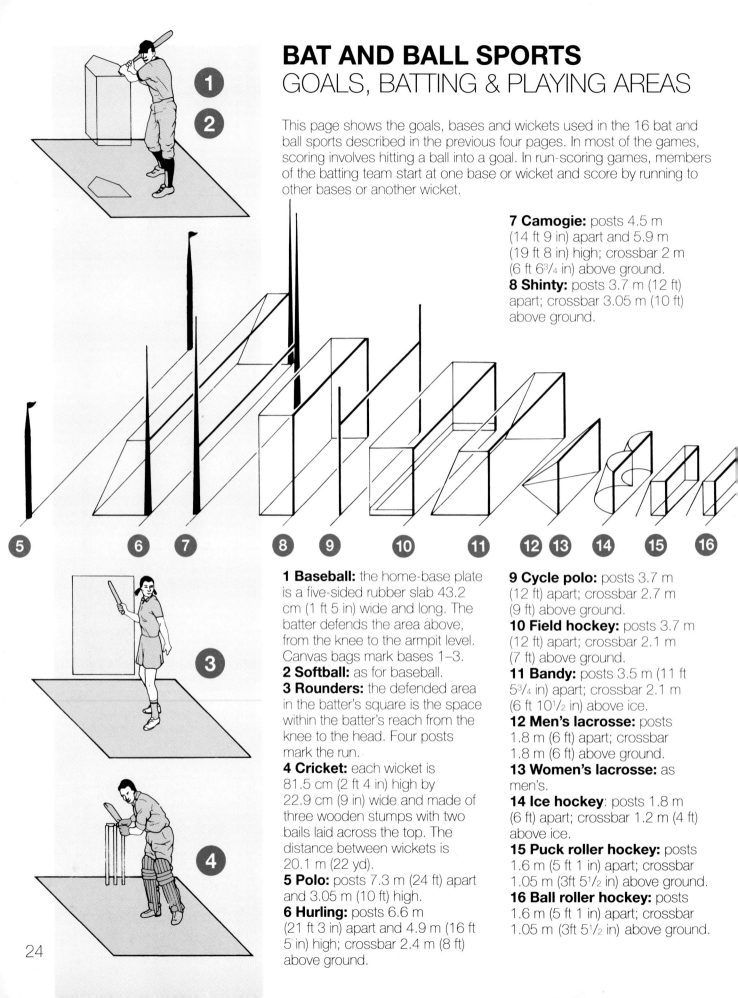

7 Camogie: posts 4.5 m (14 ft 9 in) apart and 5.9 m (19 ft 8 in) high; crossbar 2 m (6 ft 6¾ in) above ground.

8 Shinty: posts 3.7 m (12 ft) apart; crossbar 3.05 m (10 ft) above ground.

1 Baseball: the home-base plate is a five-sided rubber slab 43.2 cm (1 ft 5 in) wide and long. The batter defends the area above, from the knee to the armpit level. Canvas bags mark bases 1–3.

2 Softball: as for baseball.

3 Rounders: the defended area in the batter's square is the space within the batter's reach from the knee to the head. Four posts mark the run.

4 Cricket: each wicket is 81.5 cm (2 ft 4 in) high by 22.9 cm (9 in) wide and made of three wooden stumps with two bails laid across the top. The distance between wickets is 20.1 m (22 yd).

5 Polo: posts 7.3 m (24 ft) apart and 3.05 m (10 ft) high.

6 Hurling: posts 6.6 m (21 ft 3 in) apart and 4.9 m (16 ft 5 in) high; crossbar 2.4 m (8 ft) above ground.

9 Cycle polo: posts 3.7 m (12 ft) apart; crossbar 2.7 m (9 ft) above ground.

10 Field hockey: posts 3.7 m (12 ft) apart; crossbar 2.1 m (7 ft) above ground.

11 Bandy: posts 3.5 m (11 ft 5¾ in) apart; crossbar 2.1 m (6 ft 10½ in) above ice.

12 Men's lacrosse: posts 1.8 m (6 ft) apart; crossbar 1.8 m (6 ft) above ground.

13 Women's lacrosse: as men's.

14 Ice hockey: posts 1.8 m (6 ft) apart; crossbar 1.2 m (4 ft) above ice.

15 Puck roller hockey: posts 1.6 m (5 ft 1 in) apart; crossbar 1.05 m (3ft 5½ in) above ground.

16 Ball roller hockey: posts 1.6 m (5 ft 1 in) apart; crossbar 1.05 m (3ft 5½ in) above ground.

Batting and Playing Areas

1 Polo:
274.5m x 146.4m
(900ft x 480ft)

2 Shinty:
146.4m x 73.2m
(480ft x 240ft)

3 Hurling:
144.9m x 90m
(475ft x 295 ft)

4 Camogie:
110m x 70m
(360ft x 229ft 8in)

5 Bandy: 109.8m x
65m (360 x 213ft)

6 Women's lacrosse:
109.8m x 64.1m
(360ft x 210ft)

7 Cycle polo:
100.7m x 73.2m
(330ft x 240ft)

8 Men's lacrosse:
100.7m x 54.9m
(330ft x 180ft)

9 Field hockey:
91.5m x 54.9m
(300ft x180ft)

10 Ice hockey:
61m x 30.5m
(200ft x 100ft)

11 Ball roller hockey:
40m x 20m
(131ft 3in x 65ft 7in)

12 Baseball: infield
diamond
27.5m x 27.5m
(90ft x 90ft)

13 Softball: infield
diamond 19.8m x
19.8m (65ft x 65ft)

14 Rounders: infield
18m x 12m
(59ft 1in x 39ft 4in)

**15 Cricket: bowling
pitch:** 20.1m x 2.5m
(66ft x 8ft 8in)

**16 Puck roller
hockey:** there are no
fixed dimensions for the
playing area

Ice

Wood

Grass

©DIAGRAM

25

Bats and Sticks

BAT AND BALL SPORTS
DRESS & PLAYING EQUIPMENT

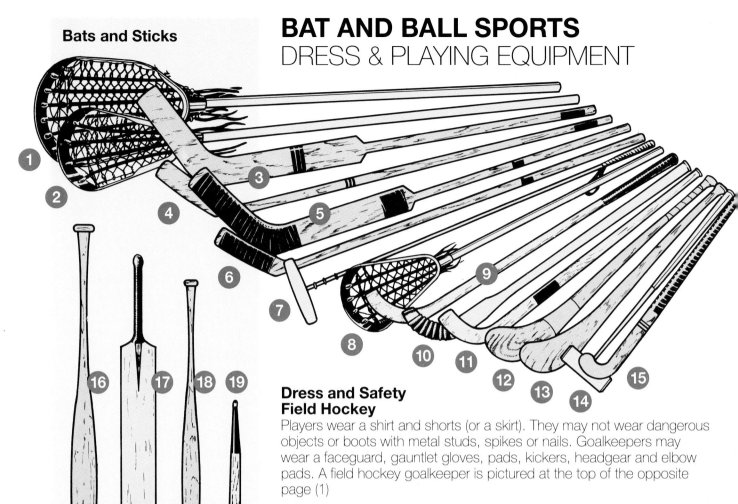

1 Men's lacrosse goalkeeper's crosse
2 Men's lacrosse player's crosse
3 Puck roller hockey goalkeeper's stick
4 Puck roller hockey player's stick
5 Ice hockey goalkeeper's stick
6 Ice hockey player's stick
7 Polo mallet
8 Women's lacrosse crosse
9 Shinty caman
10 Bandy stick
11 Ball roller hockey stick
12 Hurling hurley
13 Camogie camog
14 Cycle polo mallet
15 Field hockey stick
16 Baseball bat
17 Cricket bat
18 Softball bat
19 Rounders bat

Dress and Safety
Field Hockey
Players wear a shirt and shorts (or a skirt). They may not wear dangerous objects or boots with metal studs, spikes or nails. Goalkeepers may wear a faceguard, gauntlet gloves, pads, kickers, headgear and elbow pads. A field hockey goalkeeper is pictured at the top of the opposite page (1)

Cricket
Players wear white or cream shirts and trousers (or a skirt), cricket boots with spiked or rubber soles, and possibly a sweater and a peaked cap. Coloured clothing is worn in some professional matches. Batsmen and wicket keepers wear gloves and leg guards, and batsmen often wear a helmet and an abdomen protector (2).

Baseball
Players wear a numbered uniform including a cap, jersey, short trousers, socks and spiked shoes. Batters wear a batting helmet. Fielders may wear a leather glove. The pictured catcher wears a catcher's mitt and protective helmet, face mask, throat guard, chest protector and knee and shin guards (3).

Ice Hockey
Players wear a numbered uniform of helmet, sweater, knee-length trousers, long socks, skates and padded gloves. Beneath the uniform are shoulder pads, elbow pads, shin guards and other items. The pictured goalkeeper has a chest protector, face mask and leg guards, a catching glove and stick-hand glove (4).

Rounders
Players usually wear a shirt, skirt, socks and trainers.

Softball
Uniforms are similar to those worn for baseball. Catchers must wear masks and women catchers must wear body protectors.

26

Lacrosse
Men wear numbered shirts, helmets, face guards, shorts or tracksuit trousers, elbow pads, gauntlets and shin guards. Goalkeepers also wear a body pad and thigh pads.

Shinty
Players wear jerseys, shorts, socks and boots without spikes or studs. The goalkeeper's jersey is a different colour from the rest.

Bandy
Players' gear includes a helmet, face mask or mouth guard, shin pads and padded gloves. Skates must not be sharply pointed. Goalkeepers wear distinctive dress with leg pads.

Hurling
Players wear a shirt, shorts, socks and boots. A helmet may be worn as well.

Roller Hockey
Players' gear includes knee pads and other protective padding, and boots with roller skates bolted on. Goalkeepers wear extra items.

Polo
Polo players usually wear a jersey and white breeches with polo boots and knee guards, and may wear gloves. All players must wear a polo helmet or cap with a chinstrap. Sharp spurs are forbidden. Polo ponies wear a saddle, bridle and bit and bandages or leg boots on all four legs. They must not be fitted with blinkers or a noseband that stops them from seeing clearly.

Cycle Polo
Clothes worn are similar to those for polo. Each team has its own colours, and players may wear a cap or a helmet, pads and boots.

Balls and Pucks
Here we show the relative sizes of 14 balls and 2 pucks used in bat and ball sports. The largest ball is the softball, up to 30.7cm (12 in) in circumference. The smallest ball is the bandy ball, 6.4 cm ($2\frac{1}{2}$ in) in diameter.

1 Softball
2 Polo
3 Cycle polo
4 Hurling
5 Field hockey
6 Baseball
7 Cricket
8 Roller hockey ball
9 Camogie
10 Lacrosse (men)
11 Lacrosse (women)
12 Shinty
13 Rounders
14 Bandy
15 Ice hockey puck
16 Roller hockey puck

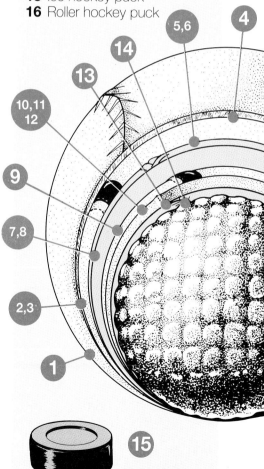

BAT AND BALL SPORTS
HALL OF FAME

Joe Dimaggio
This great baseball player won the American League batting championship in 1939 and 1940. In 1941, he set a record making one or more base hits in 56 consecutive games. Altogether he helped to lead the New York Yankees to nine world championships. In 1955, he was elected to the National Baseball Hall of Fame.

Babe Ruth
Baseball's first great hitter of home runs set 76 batting and pitching baseball records in his 22-year career (1914– 35). His 60 home runs in a season (1927) was unbeaten for more than 30 years. Altogether he scored 714 home runs, playing in 2,502 games. In 1936, he was elected to the National Baseball Hall of Fame.

Women Cricketers
The highest score in women's test cricket was 193 runs hit by Denise Annetts for Australia against England in 1987. Her 309 partnership with Lindsay Reeler was a record too. England's Rachel Heyhoe-Flint played the most tests (25) and scored the most runs (1,814) in a test career (from 1960 to 1979).

W. G. Grace
Dr William Gilbert ('W. G.') Grace is probably the most famous cricketer of all time. This burly figure with the spade-shaped beard dominated English cricket in the last part of the nineteenth century. He broke almost all existing records in a career in first-class cricket that lasted from 1865 to 1908. As a batsman, he scored more than 54,900 runs, including 126 centuries. In 1871, he set a record of 2,736 runs in a single season. His highest innings score was 344 in 1876. As a bowler, he took more than 2,870 wickets. As a fielder, he caught batsmen out more than 870 times.

Grace played long after most cricketers would have retired. In his last match, aged 66, he scored 69 not out.

Sean Kerly

In the 1980s, this British player developed into one of the great goal scorers of field hockey. In 1984, his seven goals contributed to Great Britain's bronze medal in the Olympic Games. In 1985, he helped his club Southgate to seize the first of four consecutive national titles. In the following year, his four goals helped England to win the World Cup silver medal. In 1987, he contributed to England's European Cup silver medal. In 1988, Kerly's eight goals helped Great Britain to win the Olympic Games field hockey final. Before the year was out, Kerly's record stood at 56 goals scored in 69 games while playing for Great Britain.

Viv Richards

In the 1970s and 1980s, West Indian cricketer Vivian ('Viv') Richards became known as the best batsman in world cricket. In 1976, in four test matches against England, he scored 829 runs for the West Indies. In 1979, his batting helped to make his team the best side in the world. In 1984, his 189 runs broke the record for a limited overs international. Captaining the West Indies in 1986, he scored the fastest ever test century. In 1988, he led the West Indies' 4–0 defeat of England, and scored his 100th century in first-class cricket.

Other Great Cricketers

Allan Border (born 1955): Australia
Geoff Boycott (born 1940): England
Don Bradman (born 1908): Australia
Martin Crowe (born 1962): New Zealand
Kapil Dev (born 1959): India
Graham Gooch (born 1953): England
David Gower (born 1957): England
Richard Hadlee (born 1951): New Zealand
Imran Khan (born 1952): Pakistan
Dennis Lillee (born 1949): Australia
Clive Lloyd (born 1944): West Indies
Rodney Marsh (born 1947): Australia
Javed Miandad (born 1957): Pakistan

Ian Botham

This big, burly English player has proved to be the terror of the cricket field. When on form, he has destroyed whole teams almost single handedly. In 1978, he became the first player to take eight wickets and score a century in a single test match (against Pakistan). In 1980, Botham broke another test record (against India) with a century and five wickets in both innings. In a 1992 World Cup match, he helped England to devastate Australia.

15 Million-dollar Man

In 1988, top-scoring ice-hockey player, Wayne Gretzky, became the costliest sportsman of all time when Los Angeles Kings bought him from Edmonton Oilers for $15 million. By then, the 27-year-old Canadian held 43 National Hockey League (NHL) records, far more than anyone before him. In 1989, in just 10 years of play, he passed the NHL record of 1850 points.

Gretzky's record season goals assists points with Edmonton Oilers:

1979/80	51	86	137
1980/81	55	109	164
1981/82	92	120	212
1982/83	71	125	196
1983/84	87	118	205
1985/86	52	163	215
1986/87	62	121	183
1987/88	40	109	149

Most Stanley Cup wins

By 1990, Montreal Canadiens won this cup 23 times. It is awarded at the annual play-off between the National Hockey League's top ice-hockey teams.

BAT AND BALL SPORTS
WOULD YOU BELIEVE?

These pages describe and list some of the outstanding records set by individuals and teams in six bat and ball sports: bandy, baseball, cricket, field hockey, ice hockey and roller hockey.
Some of the personal and team records date from recent years, but others have remained unbroken for more than half a century. It is difficult to imagine anyone bettering some of the achievements of such sportsmen as Wayne Gretzky and Don Bradman. Yet, who knows? In time, perhaps, their records, too, will fall.

Six Sixes

Batting for Nottinghamshire against Glamorgan in August 1968, the great West Indian cricketer Gary Sobers hit six consecutive balls beyond the boundary.

Sixty Thousand Runs

Between 1905 and 1934 English batsman Jack Hobbs set unbroken first-class cricket records with 61,237 runs and 197 centuries.

Zimbabwe Victory

In 1980, Zimbabwe's team became the first winners of an Olympic gold medal for women's field hockey.

Field Hockey Giants

Between 1928 and 1968 the men's field hockey Olympic final was won by either India or Pakistan. India won eight times and Pakistan won twice (in 1960 and 1968).

Fastest Centuries in Test Cricket

1 Jack Gregory (Australia): 100 runs in 70 minutes in 1921
2 Vivian Richards (West Indies): 100 runs in 81 minutes in 1986
3 Don Bradman (Australia): 200 runs in 214 minutes in 1930
4 Ian Botham (England): 200 runs in 268 minutes in 1982
5 Walter Hammond (England): 300 runs in 288 minutes in 1933

Mike Schmidt

This Philadelphia baseball player broke the National League record for the number of seasons as top scorer of home runs (clear runs right around the diamond or infield). He made the highest score eight times: 1974, 1975, 1976, 1980, 1981, 1983, 1984 and 1986. Also, six times he scored more home runs than any other National League or American League player: 1974 (36 home runs), 1975 (38), 1976 (38), 1980 (48), 1981 (31) and 1983 (40).

Jim Laker

Bowling for England against Australia in 1956, Jim Laker took 10 wickets for 53 runs in an innings, and 19 for 90 in the match. These test records remain unbroken.

Top Baseball Team

The New York Yankees won the World Series 22 times between 1923 and 1978 and they were runners-up 11 times. This team holds the record for the most wins and the most appearances.

Sunil Gavaskar

Between 1971 and 1987, this Indian cricketer set three records. **1** Most test matches: 125. **2** Most runs in a test career: 10,122. **3** Most test centuries: 34.

Don Bradman

Between 1929 and 1948, this Australian cricketer set test match batting records, some of which still stand. Playing against England in 1930, he became the first to score 300 runs in a test and remains the only man to reach 300 in a day. Not only did he score 974 runs in the same test series, he scored 100 centuries in fewer than 300 innings. No one has come close to Bradman's average test cricket score of 99.9 runs.

77 Runs Off One Over

In 1990, a Shell Trophy cricket match in New Zealand between Wellington and Canterbury produced 77 runs off one over. Wellington's Bert Vance deliberately bowled easy balls and no-balls to Lee German who hit 70 runs (including eight sixes and five fours) and Richard Petrie, who scored 5 runs (one four and a single). Two no-balls made up the other two runs. Altogether, Vance bowled 17 deliberate no-balls and only five good balls, so the six-ball over finished one ball short.

Roller Hockey

By 1990, Portugal was the top team. It had won the World Championship 12 times (1947–50, 1952, 1956, 1958, 1960, 1962, 1968, 1974 and 1982). Between 1947 and 1987, Portugal had also won the European Championship 16 times. In both contests, Spain is the next most frequent winner.

Bandy

Between 1961 and 1977, Valeriy Maslov of the USSR was a World Championship gold medal winner eight times: in 1961, 1963, 1965, 1967, 1971, 1973, 1975 and 1977.

Save Your Breath

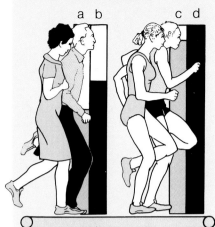

Athletes use more of the oxygen they breathe in than ordinary people use. Measuring the pulse and breathing rates of people running on a treadmill shows the body's oxygen uptake. This is given in millilitres of oxygen per kilogram of body weight per minute. Here, the maximum oxygen uptake is shown of (**a**) an average woman, 40 ml/kg/min; (**b**) an average man, 52 ml/kg/min; (**c**) a female athlete, 68 ml/kg/min; and (**d**) a male athlete, 75 ml/kg/min.

Oxygen Use

The more vigorous the exercise, the more oxygen the body needs.
Below we compare the relative demands for oxygen produced by 30 minutes' participation in various sports.

Wrestling ●●●●●●
●●●●●●●
Ice hockey ●●●●●
Handball ●●●●●
Squash ●●●●●
Basketball ●●●●
Skiing ●●●
Soccer ●●●
Lacrosse ●●●
Tennis ●●●
American football ●●●
Volleyball ●●
Skating ●●
Golf ●

BODY MACHINES

1	2	3	4	5
Archery	**Cricket**	**Baseball**	Ice skating	**Touchball**
Boules	**Polo**	Canoeing	Long jump	**Volleyball**
Fishing	**Softball**	Equestrian	Sprint	Alpine skiing
Golf	Bobsleigh	three-day	cycling	Badminton
Pool	racing	eventing	Surfing	Fencing
Powerboat	Diving	Motor racing	Tug-of-War	Hammer
racing	Javelin	Motorcycle	Weight lifting	Horse racing
Snooker	Roller-	racing		(flat)
Water-skiing	skating	Scuba diving		Karate
	Shot put			Pole vault
	Table tennis			
	Tenpin			
	bowling			
	Yacht			
	racing			

Overall Ratings

When working, to a greater or lesser degree, the body uses up food and oxygen to release energy. Various researchers have calculated the different demands that are made on the body by different sports. Above, one such rating, on a scale from 1 to 10, is shown. The sports described in this book are in bold print. The higher the figure, the more demanding the sport. Remember, though, that this kind of rating is not exact, and some people work at a sport much harder than other people.

Heart–lung System

To work steadily, muscles need an efficient heart–lung system. The lungs supply blood with oxygen and remove waste gas. The heart pumps oxygen-rich blood from the lungs to the muscles to help them to work. It also pumps blood, containing waste gas, from the muscles to the lungs. Athletes can check their heart–lung efficiency with the Harvard step test. They step up and down a 51 cm (20 in) step 30 times a minute for 5 minutes. They measure their pulse rates before, during and after the test. The results produce the index shown on the right. The higher the score, the greater the effort to which the heart–lung system is accustomed.

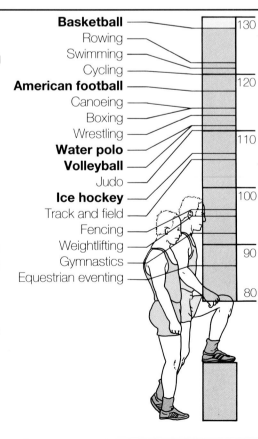

Basketball — 130
Rowing —
Swimming —
Cycling — 120
American football —
Canoeing —
Boxing —
Wrestling — 110
Water polo —
Volleyball —
Judo —
Ice hockey — 100
Track and field —
Fencing —
Weightlifting — 90
Gymnastics —
Equestrian eventing — 80

Field hockey Lacrosse Cross country running Gymnastics Hurdling Relay racing Swimming Tennis Trampolining	American football Ice hockey Rugby Soccer Water polo High jump Judo Mountain climbing Sprinting Squash	Basketball Handball Pentathlon Wrestling	Boxing Marathon Nordic skiing	Tour de France cycling
				Decathlon
6	**7**	**8**	**9**	**10** **10+**

Bodywork

Different sports make demands on different parts of the body. The chart below shows the demands made by various sports on muscular strength, endurance and mobility.

Key Muscle strength = △ Muscle endurance = ■ Mobility and flexibility = ▲

Sport	Shoulders	Back	Trunk	Arms	Legs
American football		△ ■	△	△	△ ■
Australian football	△ ■ ▲				△ ■ ▲
Baseball	▲			▲	▲
Basketball					△ ■ ▲
Boxing		△ ■	△ ■	△ ■ ▲	△ ■ ▲
Cricket	▲			▲	△ ▲
Fencing				▲	△ ▲
Field hockey		■		▲	△ ■ ▲
Gymnastics	△ ■ ▲	△	△	△ ■ ▲	△ ▲
Handball	▲			△ ▲	△ ■ ▲
High jump		△	△		△
Ice hockey		△	△	△	△ ■
Judo		△ ■	△ ■	△ ■ ▲	△ ■ ▲
Karate		△ ■	△ ■	△ ■ ▲	△ ■ ▲
Lacrosse	▲			△ ■ ▲	△ ■ ▲
Long jump		△	△		△ ▲
Pole vault	△ ▲	△ ▲	△ ▲	△ ▲	△ ▲
Rowing	△ ■	△ ■	△ ■ ▲	■	△ ■
Rugby				△	△ ■ ▲
Soccer					△ ■ ▲
Speedball					△ ■ ▲
Sprinting					△ ▲
Squash	△ ▲			△ ▲	△ ■ ▲
Swimming	△ ■ ▲	△ ■	△ ■	△ ■ ▲	△ ■ ▲
Tennis	△ ▲			△ ▲	△ ▲
Throwing events	△ ■ ▲	△		△ ▲	△ ▲
Volleyball	▲			△ ■ ▲	△ ■
Water polo	▲	■	■	△ ■	■
Water-skiing	△ ■	■	■	△ ■	△ ■
Weightlifting	△ ■	△ ■	△ ■	△ ■	△ ■
Wrestling	△ ■ ▲	△ ■ ▲	△ ■ ▲	△ ■ ▲	△ ■ ▲

Heart Size

Heart size shows the physical demands of different sports. Measuring the heart sizes of different athletes has helped to produce a heart size index. The higher the index number, shown below, the more steadily strenuous the activity.

24.8 Tour de France cyclists
21.5 Marathon runners
20.5 Long-distance runners
19.3 Rowers
18.9 Boxers
18.1 Sprint cyclists
18.1 Middle-distance runners
17.6 Weightlifters
16.4 Swimmers
16.0 Sprinters
15.7 Decathletes

Calorie Consumption

Food energy is measured in kilocalories. The more energy a sport demands, the more kilocalories you need. Below are shown the kilocalories per hour used by athletes taking part in different sports. Each dot equals 100 kilocalories. The more dots, the more strenuous the sport.

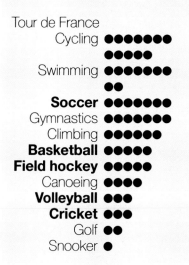

Tour de France
Cycling ●●●●●● ●●●●●
Swimming ●●●●●●● ●●
Soccer ●●●●●●
Gymnastics ●●●●●●●
Climbing ●●●●●●
Basketball ●●●●●
Field hockey ●●●●●
Canoeing ●●●●
Volleyball ●●●
Cricket ●●●
Golf ●●
Snooker ●

USEFUL ADDRESSES

UK and Eire

Sports information bodies

British Olympic Association
1 Church Row
Wandsworth Plain
London SW18 1EH

International Assembly of National
Confederations of Sport
Francis House
Francis Street
London SW1P 1DE

The Sports Council Information
  Centre
16 Upper Woburn Place
London WC1H 0QP

Baseball

British Baseball Federation
East Park Lido
Hull HU8 9AV

Basketball

English Basketball Association
Calomax House
Lupton Avenue
Leeds LS9 6EE

Canoe sports

British Canoe Union
Mappereley Hall
Lucknow Avenue
Nottingham NG3 5FA

Cricket

Marylebone Cricket Club
Lord's Ground
London NW8 8QN

Field hockey

The Hockey Association
16 Northdown Street
London N1 9BG

Gaelic football

Cumann Luthchleas Gael
Parc an Chrocaigh
Ath Cliath 3
Dublin 3

Hurling

Gaelic Athletic Association (Eire)
Croke Park
Dublin 3

Korfball

British Korfball Association
PO Box 179
Maidstone
Kent ME14 1LU

Lacrosse

English Lacrosse Union
70 High Road
Rayleigh
Essex SS6 7AD

All England Women's Lacrosse
  Association
Francis House
Francis Street
London SW1P 1DE

Netball

All England Netball Association Ltd
Francis House
Francis Street
London SW1P 1DE

Polo

The Hurlingham Polo Association
Ambersham Farm
Ambersham
Midhurst
West Sussex GU29 0BX

Roller hockey

National Roller Hockey Association of
England
528 Loose Road
Maidstone
Kent ME15 9UF

Rounders

National Rounders Association
110 Broadmead Road
Woodford Green
Essex 1G8 7EH

Rugby

Rugby Football Union
Rugby Road
Twickenham
London TW1 1DZ

The British Amateur Rugby League
Association (BARLA)
West Yorkshire House
4 New North Parade
Huddersfield HD1 5JP

Shinty

Camanachd Association
Algare
Badabrie
Banavie
Fort William PH33 7LX

Soccer

The Football Association Ltd
16 Lancaster Gate
London W2 3LW

Softball

National Softball Federation
PO Box 1303
London NW3 5TU

Team handball

British Handball Association
Bridgefield Forum Leisure Centre
Cantbridge Lane
Halewood
Liverpool L26 6LH

Volleyball

English Volleyball Association
27 South Road
West Bridgford
Nottingham NG2 7AG

Water polo

Amateur Swimming Association
Harold Fern House
Derby Square
Loughborough LE11 0AL

Australia

Australian rules football

Australian Football League
120 Jolimont Road
Jolimont
Victoria 3002

Basketball

National Basketball League
209 Toorak Road
Soutn Yarra
Victoria 3141

Cricket

Australian Cricket Board
70 Jolimont Road
Jolimont
Victoria 3002

Rugby league

NSW Rugby League
165 Phillip Street
Sydney
NSW 2000

Rugby union

Australian Rugby Union
353 Anzac Parade
Kingsford
NSW 2032

South Africa

Rugby Union

South African Rugby Union
Boundry Road
Newlands Rugby Ground
Newlands
Cape Town 7700

Cricket

United Cricket Board Union
PO Box 55009
Northlands
Johannesburg 2116

INDEX

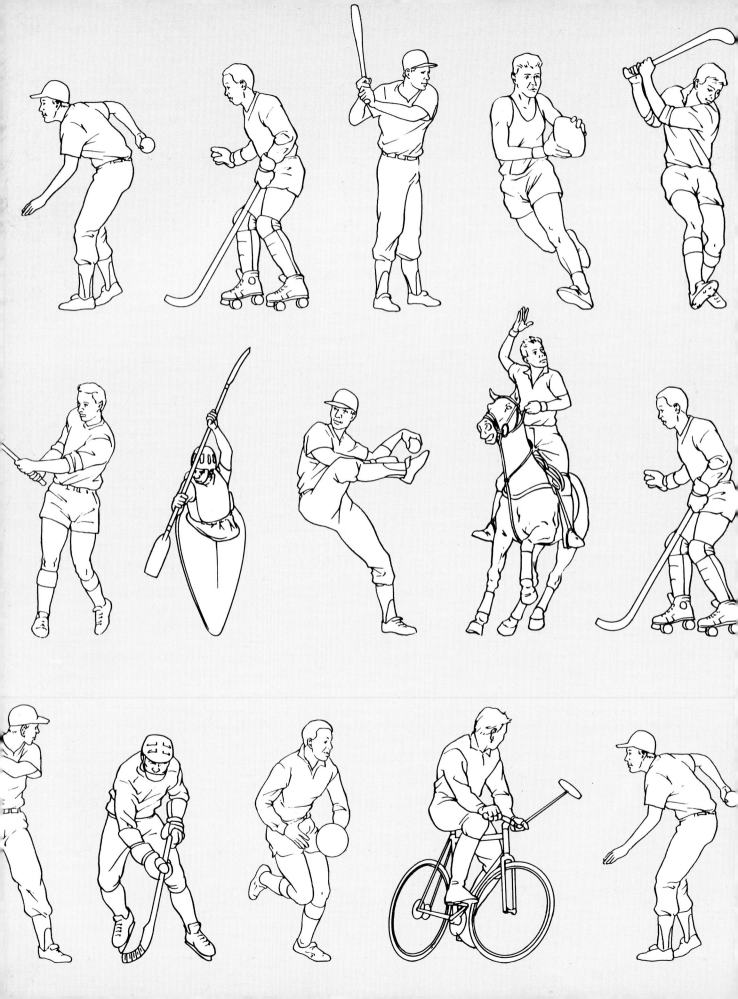